Animals For Beginners Coloring Book

Other popular books by **(Sonali Hossen)** Which can give gifts to your loved ones or Any guy. Honestly, our products are very good, and popular!

What challenge did you face to color the picture?

Sub..Date..................

What challenge did you face to color the picture?

Sub..Date...................

What challenge did you face to color the picture?

Sub...Date....................

What challenge did you face to color the picture?

Sub..Date...................

What challenge did you face to color the picture?

Sub...................................Date..................

What challenge did you face to color the picture?

Sub..Date....................

What challenge did you face to color the picture?

Sub..Date.................

What challenge did you face to color the picture?

Sub..Date..................

What challenge did you face to color the picture?

Sub..Date..................

What challenge did you face to color the picture?

Sub...Date...................

What challenge did you face to color the picture?

Sub................................Date.................

What challenge did you face to color the picture?

Sub..Date..................

What challenge did you face to color the picture?

Sub..Date..................

What challenge did you face to color the picture?

Sub..Date..................

What challenge did you face to color the picture?

Sub..Date...................

What challenge did you face to color the picture?

Sub..Date...................

What challenge did you face to color the picture?

Sub......................................Date..................

What challenge did you face to color the picture?

Sub..Date..................

What challenge did you face to color the picture?

Sub...Date..................

Sub..Date..................

What challenge did you face to color the picture?

Sub..Date...................

Sub..Date..................

What challenge did you face to color the picture?

Sub.................................Date...................

What challenge did you face to color the picture?

Sub...Date....................

What challenge did you face to color the picture?

Sub...Date...................

What challenge did you face to color the picture?

Sub..Date..................

What challenge did you face to color the picture?

Sub..Date...................

What challenge did you face to color the picture?

Sub..Date...................

Sub..Date...................

What challenge did you face to color the picture?

Sub..Date..................

What challenge did you face to color the picture?

Sub...Date...................

What challenge did you face to color the picture?

Sub......................................**Date**..................

What challenge did you face to color the picture?

Sub...Date...................

What challenge did you face to color the picture?

Sub..Date.................

What challenge did you face to color the picture?

Sub...Date...................

Sub...Date...................

What challenge did you face to color the picture?

Sub.. Date..................

What challenge did you face to color the picture?

Sub..Date...................

What challenge did you face to color the picture?

Sub...Date....................

What challenge did you face to color the picture?

Sub.......................................Date....................

What challenge did you face to color the picture?

Sub..Date...................

What challenge did you face to color the picture?

Sub..................................Date...................

What challenge did you face to color the picture?

Sub...Date...................

What challenge did you face to color the picture?

Sub..Date...................

Sub.. Date..................

What challenge did you face to color the picture?

Sub...Date....................

What challenge did you face to color the picture?

Sub...Date...................

www.ingramcontent.com/pod-product-compliance
Lightning Source LLC
Chambersburg PA
CBHW081733250726
48657CB00010B/3250